Amazing
Insects

WRITTEN BY
LAURENCE MOUND

PHOTOGRAPHED BY
FRANK GREENAWAY

Dorling Kindersley Education
London • New York • Stuttgart

A Dorling Kindersley Education Book

Editor Bernadette Crowley
Art editor Hans Verkroost
Assistant editor David Fung
Managing editor Sophie Mitchell
Managing art editor Miranda Kennedy
Production Shelagh Gibson

Illustrations by Mark Iley, Julie Anderson and John Hutchinson
Insects photographed on location in Belize, Central America.
The publishers would like to thank the Programme for
Belize, which helped us find and photograph the insects.
Programme for Belize is a non-profit-making organization
working to preserve the natural beauty of Belize, which has
extensive tropical rainforests.

Giraffe weevils (pp. 28-29) photographed at the Natural History Museum, London

This is a Dorling Kindersley Education edition, 1994

First published in Great Britain in 1993 by
Dorling Kindersley Limited,
9 Henrietta Street, London, WC2E 8PS

A CIP catalogue record for this book
is available from the British Library

ISBN 0-7513-5025-7 (trade edition)
ISBN 0-7516-0364-3 (school edition)

Colour reproduction by Colourscan, Singapore
Printed in Italy by A. Mondadori Editore, Verona

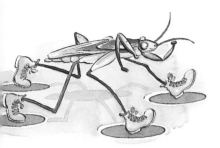

Contents

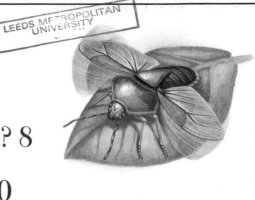

Throughout the book, a child's hand is used as a measure to show you the size of the insects in the main pictures.

What is an insect?

There are thought to be about five million different kinds of insects in the world. Insects have no skeleton inside them; their skin is their skeleton. The skin is tough and protects and supports the body like a suit of armour.

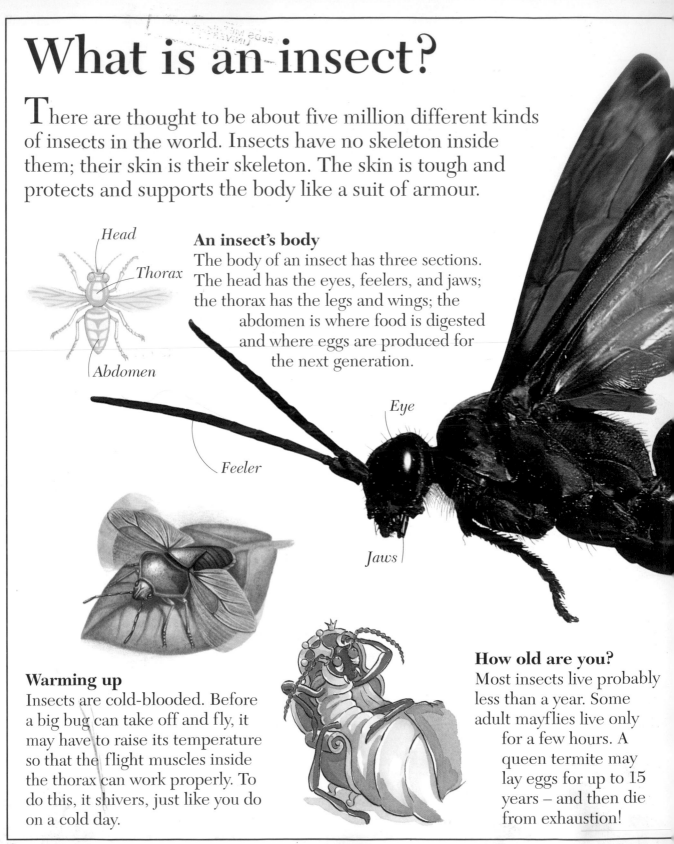

Head

Thorax

Abdomen

An insect's body
The body of an insect has three sections. The head has the eyes, feelers, and jaws; the thorax has the legs and wings; the abdomen is where food is digested and where eggs are produced for the next generation.

Eye

Feeler

Jaws

Warming up
Insects are cold-blooded. Before a big bug can take off and fly, it may have to raise its temperature so that the flight muscles inside the thorax can work properly. To do this, it shivers, just like you do on a cold day.

How old are you?
Most insects live probably less than a year. Some adult mayflies live only for a few hours. A queen termite may lay eggs for up to 15 years – and then die from exhaustion!

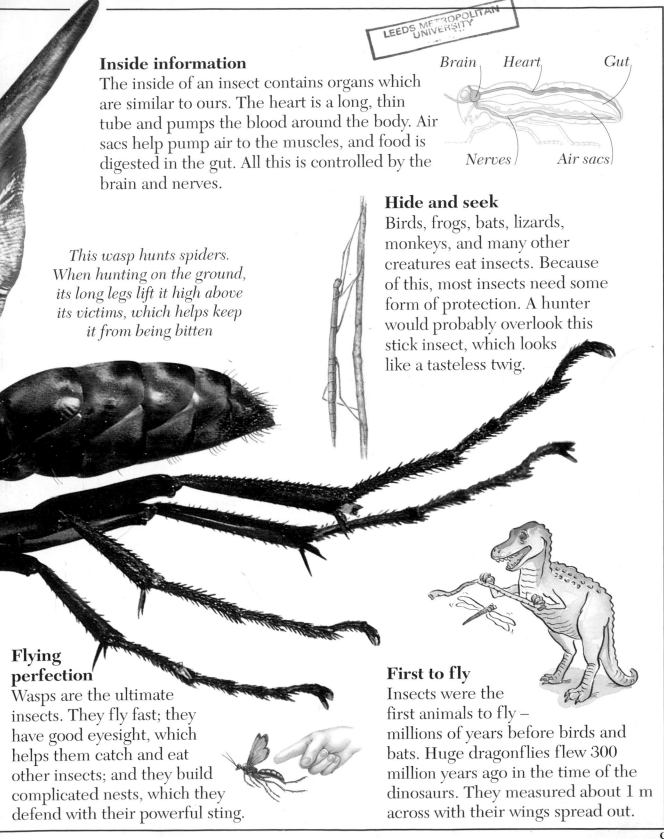

Inside information

The inside of an insect contains organs which are similar to ours. The heart is a long, thin tube and pumps the blood around the body. Air sacs help pump air to the muscles, and food is digested in the gut. All this is controlled by the brain and nerves.

Brain   Heart   Gut

Nerves   Air sacs

This wasp hunts spiders. When hunting on the ground, its long legs lift it high above its victims, which helps keep it from being bitten

Hide and seek

Birds, frogs, bats, lizards, monkeys, and many other creatures eat insects. Because of this, most insects need some form of protection. A hunter would probably overlook this stick insect, which looks like a tasteless twig.

Flying perfection

Wasps are the ultimate insects. They fly fast; they have good eyesight, which helps them catch and eat other insects; and they build complicated nests, which they defend with their powerful sting.

First to fly

Insects were the first animals to fly – millions of years before birds and bats. Huge dragonflies flew 300 million years ago in the time of the dinosaurs. They measured about 1 m across with their wings spread out.

9

Growing up

Some insects hatch from the egg looking like miniature adults – these young are called nymphs. Others hatch as larvae – small, wingless creatures which look very different from the adults.

Ladybird eggs   *Larva*   *Pupa*   *Adult ladybird*

The change of life
There are four stages of growth for ladybirds and most other insects. They start as an egg. They hatch from the egg as a larva. The larva feeds and grows until it becomes a pupa. Inside the pupa the body changes into an adult insect.

Female holding insect

Not such a good mate
When meat-eating insects mate, a male is in danger of becoming his wife's next meal. A male empid fly avoids this by giving a female another insect to eat while he mates with her.

Caterpillar

Butterfly

Double life
Insect larvae often lead a different life from adult insects. Butterfly larvae, called caterpillars, spend their days eating leaves. Butterfly adults flutter around drinking nectar from flowers, mating, and laying eggs.

New skin

Old skin being shed

Changing armour
An insect's outside skeleton, or skin, does not grow as the insect grows. The insect must shed its skin and grow a new, bigger skin several times from egg to adult.

Hatching

Some insects hatch looking like miniature adults. This assassin bug is coming out of its egg. It will be an adult after growing and shedding its skin several times.

Egg

Why bother mating?

Mating is slow and sometimes dangerous. Aphids mate in the autumn. But in the summer, female aphids don't need the males – they can produce young without mating.

Good protection

Treehoppers and their nymphs live in groups on plants. They feed on plant juices and produce a sweet liquid called honeydew, which ants love to drink. The ants protect the treehoppers from enemies in return for their favourite drink!

Treehopper nymphs live in separate groups from the adults

Adult treehoppers are disguised as plant thorns

Senses

We do not really know what an insect feels, but we do know that insects can see, smell, and hear some things which we cannot.

Fantastic feelers

Insects do not have a nose: they smell with their feelers. The feathery feelers of the silkworm moth can smell the scent of a female more than four kilometres away.

Wash and brush-up

A speck of dust which we can hardly see will cover the tiny eyes of an insect. If you watch a fly, you will see it wipe its eyes with its front legs every few seconds.

Making contact

Some cave crickets have feelers five times as long as their bodies. This helps them to feel their way around in the dark of a cave, to find food and water – and each other.

Tiny eyes form one big eye

Big eyes

Hunting insects, such as dragonflies, have big eyes which are made up of thousands of tiny eyes. Dragonflies can spot the movement of another insect up to 10 metres away, but their eyes cannot focus on details the way our eyes can.

Ear

Ear on the knee

Crickets have their ears on their front legs, just beneath their knees!

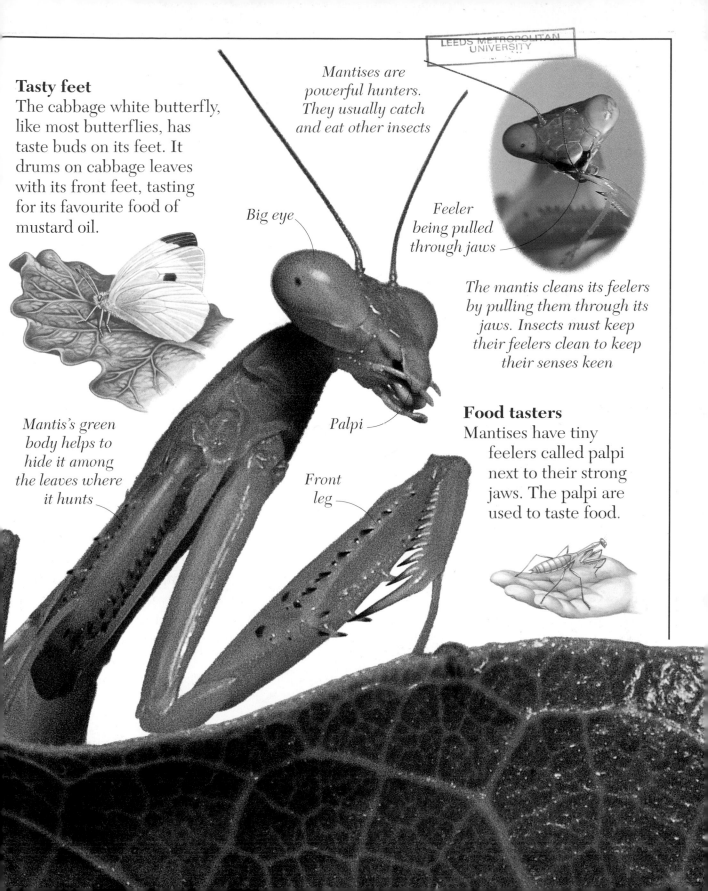

Tasty feet
The cabbage white butterfly, like most butterflies, has taste buds on its feet. It drums on cabbage leaves with its front feet, tasting for its favourite food of mustard oil.

Mantises are powerful hunters. They usually catch and eat other insects

Big eye

Feeler being pulled through jaws

The mantis cleans its feelers by pulling them through its jaws. Insects must keep their feelers clean to keep their senses keen

Mantis's green body helps to hide it among the leaves where it hunts

Palpi

Front leg

Food tasters
Mantises have tiny feelers called palpi next to their strong jaws. The palpi are used to taste food.

Sounds & signals

Insects signal each other, and other animals, in a variety of ways. But as we do not speak their language, we can sometimes only guess at the meaning of their messages.

Loves to dance

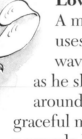

A male fruit fly uses his wings to wave at a female as he slowly dances around her. His graceful movements persuade her to mate with him.

Going in circles

Ants mark their trails with a smelly chemical, and they follow the smell. One day, several thousand ants had their trail upset by heavy rain. They were seen following each other in a circle for over 30 hours – until they all dropped dead from exhaustion.

Flashing lights

In warm countries, male and female fireflies attract each other with flashes of light. Each species uses a different pattern of flashes and colour.

"Flags" on back legs

Beating drum

When male cicadas are in the mood for romance, they sing to attract a mate by vibrating two drum-like organs in their abdomen.

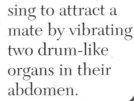

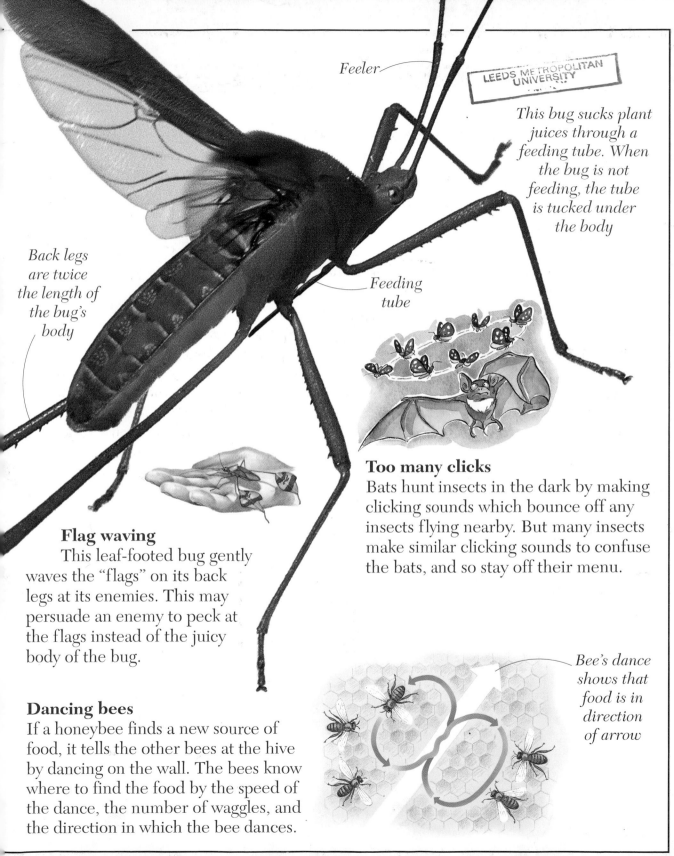

Feeler

This bug sucks plant juices through a feeding tube. When the bug is not feeding, the tube is tucked under the body

Back legs are twice the length of the bug's body

Feeding tube

Too many clicks
Bats hunt insects in the dark by making clicking sounds which bounce off any insects flying nearby. But many insects make similar clicking sounds to confuse the bats, and so stay off their menu.

Flag waving
This leaf-footed bug gently waves the "flags" on its back legs at its enemies. This may persuade an enemy to peck at the flags instead of the juicy body of the bug.

Dancing bees
If a honeybee finds a new source of food, it tells the other bees at the hive by dancing on the wall. The bees know where to find the food by the speed of the dance, the number of waggles, and the direction in which the bee dances.

Bee's dance shows that food is in direction of arrow

15

Creepy-crawlies

Running and walking are not the only things insects do with their legs. They also use them to jump and dig, to catch their food, and even to sing songs with.

Running hot
The Namib beetle, which lives in the Namib Desert, has very long legs. The legs lift its body high as it runs over scorching sand.

Going for a walk
Ants may walk 300 metres from their nest to gather food, which is a very long way for their size. It is like you walking 60 km to get the shopping! They then have to carry the food, which may be an insect as heavy as themselves, back to the nest.

Upside down
Many insects cannot grip smooth surfaces, such as windows, with their claws. But the feet of houseflies have a pad which is like plastic film, and can cling to the smoothest surface.

Pad

Claw

Although the cricket is brightly coloured, it is difficult to spot when it is among the shiny leaves of the forest trees

Colourful cricket
When this Central American cricket is disturbed by a hunter, it can leap into the air using its powerful back legs. While in mid-air, it can open its wings and fly away from danger.

The cricket is cleaning a feeler with its mouth

Legs for lunging

The praying mantis uses its front legs like a trap. It sits still on a plant waiting for some other insect to come near, then lunges forwards to snap it up and eat it.

Legs for digging

Mole crickets have large, flat front legs, similar to the front legs of a mole. They fly around on warm nights, but they can tunnel underground as quickly as a mole.

The upper part of the back legs has large muscles for long leaps

Song of love

Male grasshoppers sing by rubbing their back legs against their front pair of wings. The male of each type of cricket sings a different song so that only the right females are attracted.

Food & feeding

Different insects eat different things. They may eat anything that is, or was, alive, including leaves, hair, wood, blood, fruit, dung, pollen – or other insects.

A full stomach

Honeypot ants are like living larders. They hang upside down from the roof of the nest with swollen abdomens full of sugary liquid. The liquid feeds the other ants in the colony when food is scarce in the dry season.

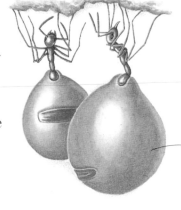

Abdomen full of liquid food

Locust swarms

Locusts live in vast colonies. A swarm of 100 million locusts will eat all the crops and plants in its path for many kilometres.

Ant gardeners

Parasol ants cut pieces of leaf and take them back to the nest. The ants seem to be carrying flags as they hold the leaves in their jaws. The leaves are used to grow a "fungus garden", on which the ants feed.

Leg

It will take the caterpillar about 1 minute to eat this leaf

Jaws are chewing on leaf

Eat, eat, eat!

Caterpillars eat non-stop in order to grow. This hawkmoth caterpillar is a high-speed eater. It could probably eat all the leaves on a small bush in a couple of days. It has grown to almost its full size and will soon pupate (turn into a pupa) to begin its magical change into a moth.

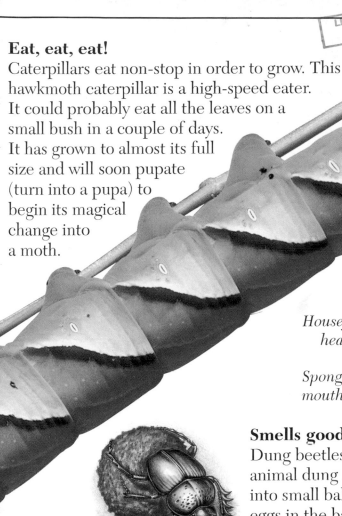

Mopping it up

Houseflies vomit on solid food. Their vomit contains juices which turn the food into a mushy liquid. They soak up this mush with their sponge-like mouthparts.

Eye

Housefly's head

Sponge-like mouthparts

Smells good!

Dung beetles collect animal dung and mould it into small balls. They lay eggs in the balls and then bury them in the ground. When the larvae hatch, they have a tasty ball of dung for their first meal!

Ball of dung

Large jaws cut into a caterpillar

Super suckers

Butterflies and moths suck up nectar from flowers through a feeding tube. When they are not feeding, the tube is coiled up under their head.

Jaws

The ground beetle uses its deadly jaws like scissors to cut into its prey. The jaws can easily chop juicy caterpillars into bite-sized pieces.

Don't eat me!

Some insects are disguised, which makes them difficult to see. Others are brightly coloured and easily seen – but they are usually poisonous. It is as if they are saying, "I dare you to eat me. If you do, you'll get sick!".

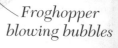

Froghopper blowing bubbles

Bubble bath

If you look closely at bushes and plants, you may see small patches of white froth. This is produced by small bugs called froghoppers. The young bugs blow bubbles from their back end, and hide in the froth.

Flying colours

This grasshopper's blotchy brown colouring makes it hard to see when it rests on the ground. But if it is disturbed, it blasts off into the air and flashes its brightly coloured underwings, which startles its enemy.

Stinkbug

The bright pink spots on this shieldbug tell birds and lizards that it tastes awful. It can also release a stinking smell which soon makes an enemy lose its appetite.

Eye

I taste awful

The black and yellow stripes of this young grasshopper warn enemies that it is poisonous. Young birds may eat a brightly coloured insect once, but they soon learn the meaning of this colourful message.

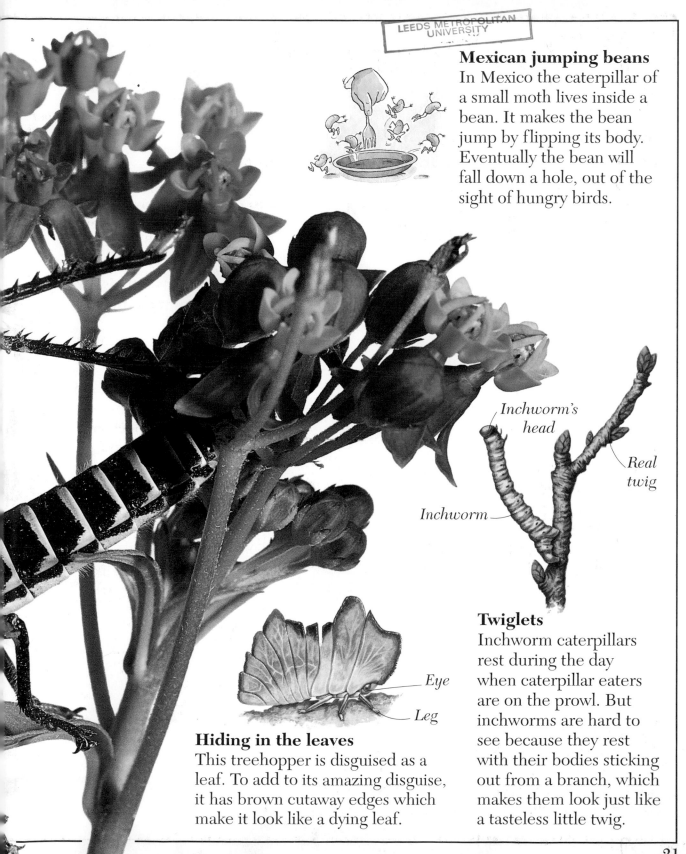

Mexican jumping beans

In Mexico the caterpillar of a small moth lives inside a bean. It makes the bean jump by flipping its body. Eventually the bean will fall down a hole, out of the sight of hungry birds.

Inchworm's head

Real twig

Inchworm

Eye

Leg

Hiding in the leaves

This treehopper is disguised as a leaf. To add to its amazing disguise, it has brown cutaway edges which make it look like a dying leaf.

Twiglets

Inchworm caterpillars rest during the day when caterpillar eaters are on the prowl. But inchworms are hard to see because they rest with their bodies sticking out from a branch, which makes them look just like a tasteless little twig.

Deadly weapons

Insects have weapons for fighting enemies and for killing other creatures for food. The weapon may be a nasty bite, a poisonous sting, or just a strong kick!

Cricket fights
Male crickets fight over females, food, and territory (living space). A fighting cricket will wrestle with its enemy and use its strong cutting jaws to try to bite the enemy to death.

These feather-like hairs pull out easily and fill the beak of any bird that pecks at them

Kicked in the teeth
An aphid looks harmless as it sucks on a rose stem. But it will use its big hind legs to kick away small wasps, which are its enemies.

Thousands of prickly spines

Safety in numbers

Processionary caterpillars have bodies which are covered in poisonous hairs. For added protection from hungry birds, they walk together in a procession (a line) which can be over 12 metres long.

A killing sting

Wasps use their powerful sting to defend themselves or their nest, and to kill other insects for food.

Stag fight

Male stag beetles fight over territory. They use their large jaws to try to turn each other over, or knock each other off a branch.

Ant terror!

Ants live in groups, and they can bite and sting, so most animals avoid them. Driver ants raid wasps' nests and steal all the wasp eggs and larvae.

Driver ants entering wasps' nest

Hairy beast

This caterpillar is covered in thick hairs and sharp spines. A hungry animal might think twice before tackling such a mouthful!

Swimmers & divers

Lots of insects live in ponds and rivers. Some walk on the bottom, some walk on the water's surface, and others dive and swim. All are looking for food – but many become the food of other water creatures.

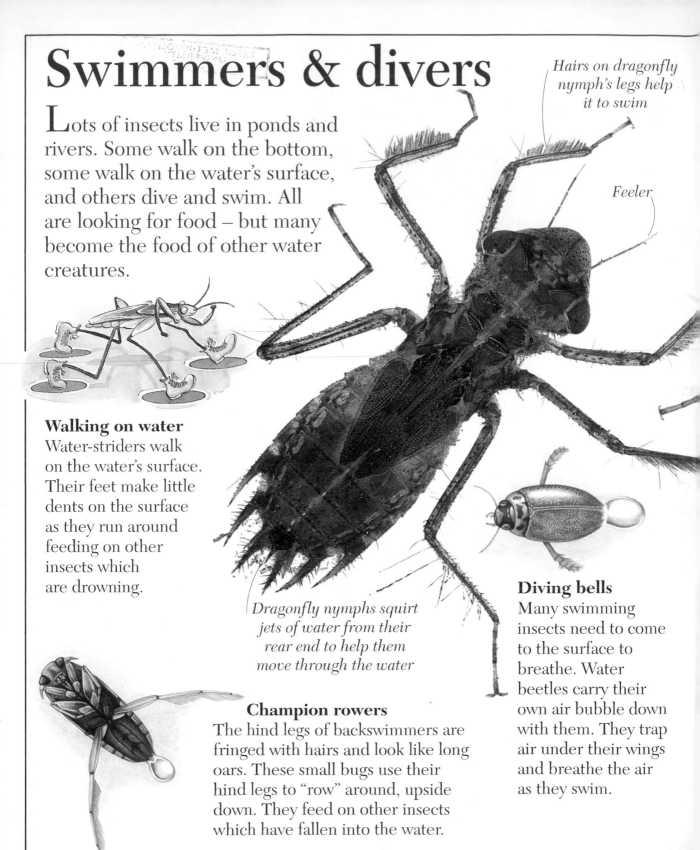

Hairs on dragonfly nymph's legs help it to swim

Feeler

Walking on water
Water-striders walk on the water's surface. Their feet make little dents on the surface as they run around feeding on other insects which are drowning.

Dragonfly nymphs squirt jets of water from their rear end to help them move through the water

Diving bells
Many swimming insects need to come to the surface to breathe. Water beetles carry their own air bubble down with them. They trap air under their wings and breathe the air as they swim.

Champion rowers
The hind legs of backswimmers are fringed with hairs and look like long oars. These small bugs use their hind legs to "row" around, upside down. They feed on other insects which have fallen into the water.

Dragonfly nymphs can be long and thin or short and fat, depending on their adult shape

Upper eye

Water level

Lower eye

Four eyes
Whirligig beetles have amazing eyes – each eye is divided into two. The upper parts spot danger above the water, whilst the lower parts keep watch underwater. Whirligigs often swim quickly in circles on the surface of a pond.

Big eyes help to spot prey in muddy water

Jutting jaws
Dragonfly nymphs live at the bottom of ponds. Their jaws are attached to a long, hinged plate which is folded beneath the head. The plate shoots forwards quickly to capture prey in front of them.

Budding wing

Top of maggot's tail above water

Dragonfly nymph is unfolding the plate, ready to snatch at its prey with its jaws

A long tail
Rat-tailed maggots live in the mud at the bottom of ponds. They breathe through their long tail, which reaches to the water's surface.

Living quarters

We have homes to protect us and in which to raise children. Many insects have similar shelters. Some insect homes contain millions of insects, and last for years; others are more temporary.

Wasp laying eggs in caterpillar

Larvae coming out of caterpillar

Adult wasp coming out of pupa

Air-conditioned nests

In West Africa, the largest termite nests, or colonies, contain up to 5 million insects. Each colony of termites builds a pointed tower several metres high. Special tunnels bring in fresh air and cooling water, and chimneys take away the heat of all those bodies.

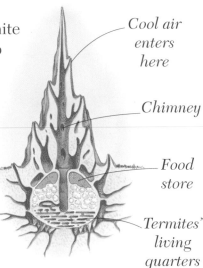

Cool air enters here

Chimney

Food store

Termites' living quarters

Bed and board

Braconid wasps lay their eggs in caterpillars. After hatching, the larvae eat the caterpillar until only the skin remains. They then become pupae, after which they will change into adult wasps.

Egg pots

A potter wasp collects mud in its jaws and makes a little pot. It places an egg inside the pot, together with a caterpillar which it has stung and paralyzed. When the larva hatches, it will feed on the still-living caterpillar.

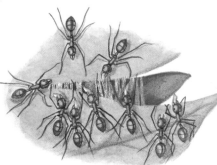

Leaf home

Weaver ants make their nests out of leaves. They pull leaves together and tie them with silk produced by the ant larvae. The adults stroke the larvae with their feelers to encourage them to spin silk.

Don't eat these apples!

Oak trees often have growths on their leaves which look like apples. The tree grows these "apples" around a spot where a gall wasp has laid its eggs. When the larvae hatch from their eggs, they feed inside the "apple".

*The wasps keep
a sharp look-out
for danger*

Keeping house

These Central American
wasps have a nest made
of paper. The wasps
make the paper by
chewing up pieces of tree
bark. The largest female
wasp lays all the eggs and
does not allow other
females to lay eggs. The
growing larvae are fed on
chewed-up caterpillars.

*Each
larva has
a separate
cell*

Egg in cell

Don't touch!

We all protect our
home, and insects
are no exception.
Remember that bees,
wasps, and ants have spent a
long time building their nests –
and they will sting to defend them.

27

Living with insects

Insects have been on Earth much longer than humans, so we have always lived with them. Some of us may think of insects as pests, but many people see them as an important part of their lives.

Sweet bees

People have eaten honey for thousands of years, but without bees, there would be no honey. Honey is made from nectar, which is found in flowers. Bees collect nectar, take it to the hive, and turn it into honey.

Nice grub

People in tropical countries eat many different insects. Australian Aborigines eat moth and beetle larvae, called witchetty grubs, which are high in protein.

Neck joint

Weird and wonderful

People have always been fascinated by insects. There are beautiful insects, such as butterflies, and strange and mysterious insects, like these giraffe weevils. Just why giraffe weevils have such long necks, nobody knows!

Wings are under the red wing cases

The giraffe weevil is a type of beetle

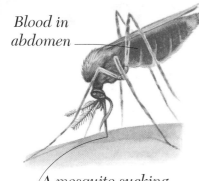

Blood in abdomen

A mosquito sucking blood through skin

Disease spreader

Mosquitos are dangerous to humans. They suck blood and can pass on the germ which causes the deadly disease malaria. Malaria is thought to kill about a million people every year.

Small world

Many insects live in your home. You may find case-bearing clothes moths in your drawers, feeding on the wool from sweaters. When they want to hide, they wind the wool around themselves, making their own matching sweaters!

The Kayapo's circular village

Being like a bee

Kayapo Indians from Brazil model their society on bee society. They think bees have the perfect way of living in harmony. Their villages are arranged like a cross-section of a beehive, with the most important hut in the middle, like the queen in the middle of a hive.

Index